WAR BETWEEN STONES AND STICKS

A WAR AND BATTLE BETWEEN THOUGHTS AND MINDSETS

ROHAN KOMPELLA

Made with ♥ on the Notion Press Platform
www.notionpress.com

I would love to dedicate this subjective script to "To the dreamer and those who dares to live."

For instance,
from ME to ME....... :)

Contents

Preface

From the very first conflict and wars,
Prayers and Weeps,
Needs and Works,
Slavery and Mastery,
Society and Country,
Religion and Race,
Attacks and Defence,
Fraud and Thefts,
Kings and Soldiers,
Citizens, and to a common individual,
Everyone does have their own thoughts regarding and basing on their own capabilities,
Sensibilities,
Opinions,
Choices and tastes.

Additionally, a few factors, such as individualism and collectivism,
does occasionally play a role while determining their goals and objectives.
This book's analysis of,
Examination of,
Discussion of,
Grasping of,
Dependence on, and
Perception of, are all related to comprehending, understanding, grasping, and perception in some way.

My capacity to perceive is completely dependent upon my ability to understand the components and sides of sociocultural and abstract aspects, which are founded on divergent beliefs, conceptions, ideas, and other realities.

Acknowledgements

For, **WAR BETWEEN STONES AND STICKS**

I'm appreciative of my brain for the many fascinating and unsettling features of the apparently endless thoughts that I always get from time to time and second to second, never understanding how or why they came to be. I am proud of myself for reading, seeing, and understanding things that were either silly or meaningless to me.

Prologue

The first word I see in my writing tools is "Begin writing here," and every time I do, I'm presented with a completely random instance and cause filled with a range of ideas and insights that I randomly consider and decide to record in any of the states or kinds of subject material it is.

In my opinion, the primary reason for writing this book is the fact that we are essentially immune to any emotional, physical, or incidental events that can affect our ability to think clearly. This book comprises a single chapter with a unified subject under the heading "What Can Be the Nonsense in This Book?" with which the subject of the consented substance begins and continues with its subjective elements considered, resembled, and connected.

"The true profession of a man is to find his way to himself"

- Hermann Hesse

Oil pastel drawing that resembles "War" inside "Brain"

THE WORLD'S

"FIRST"

NON-FICTION BOOK

WITH

JUST

"ONE CHAPTER"

CHAPTER I

War between STONES and STICKS

WAR BETWEEN STONES AND STICKS, Aside from a partial thesis of observant observations about a conflict that no one could see, the whole title is a claim made by metophar that I advanced.

I fully think that **Stones**, despite their shape and nature, can support adequate weight. I made a comparison between this and emotional thought and deliberation, which frequently do not call for a structured arrangement and can be stacked on top of one another informally or more obviously as stone-on-stone. I thought that this resemblance was sufficient due to the potent combination of the emotional components and an identical reference of likeness with the instrument.

Here, **STICK** is a sensation that we have and it has the same potential for access as placing one's hands on someone else.

Two sticks mounted on onto one another will only result in a crumbling structure in the end.

Therefore, in this context, "STONE" refers to feelings and emotions, while "STICKS" refers to reason or intellect, both of which are available inside the boundaries of the brain and the inclusion of the term WAR do have it's own confinement of definiton which is general to be known as a protracted battle between two or more parties, most often states or nations.

Wars can begin for a variety of reasons, including territorial disputes, ideological differences, or a lack of resources.

I reloaded my mental gun and chose from among all the available ammo one cartridge marked "IDEOLOGICAL DIFFERENCES" in order to aim for understanding. Since and for the reason that "WAR between STONES and STICKS" did make its strike beneath the layer of my scalp, aside from the deliberate cause, I put up with it and suffered it until this publishing.

Therefore, up to the moment you are reading these words in this book, this conflict between passion and reason has divided humanity. I have always like debating topics that combine logic, intellect, and emotional since it allows me to listen to each of them more carefully and comprehend the main ideas and arguments made.

What can be the nonsense in this book?

It is never the intention of the writing in this book to make any empty assertions that have no prospect of having any impact at all. The aim of this literary creation is to understand the core of philosophy rather than to develop any workable philosophy; **every philosophy hated is the exact same philosophy practised**. I never engaged in work that was designed to disprove or strengthen certain views, and I regard those activities as uninteresting and pointless.

In reference to numerous writing collections and understandings written by various authors of various books and by various individuals, I did hear and read many statements that were ignorant of the true purpose of the writings, and I was surprised that the writings that were intended to cause and for which they were intended to serve were misunderstood.

According to Nietzsche,

Philosophical systems are only fully true for the people

who founded them in terms of their philosophical elements that they do follow,

Then whats the point of having a social or societical philosophy?

To make things happen and work out, we use a few thought-processing tricks as well as our personal philosophical practises, convictions, or anything else that can make things so bad that nothing else can be done.

With the publication of my script, I continue to demonstrate my level of understanding and cognitive processing of the complexities and things with varied material stuffed up from the rough to the final edit level. Although every word has a definition, no two individuals will ever use the same definition in the same context.

Usually, there are only slight variances. If you write a book, all those little differences may add up, yet nobody will receive it the same. Only the individual who chose the words is aware of the true total.

Using the release of my script, I was able to show my level of knowledge and cognitive processing of the difficulties and many things using material that ranged from the rough to the final edit levels. No two people will ever use the same definition of a word in the same context, despite the fact that every word has a definition.

There are often just minor variations.

All those minor variations may add up if you create a book, but no one will read it the same way. The real total is only known to the person who picked the words.

This written publication contains a weight that requires mental calculation in addition to its technical and practical weights.

Attacking the Defence

From a predator attacking a prey to a country being attacked,
hostile nature has always taken the initiative and won the upper hand everywhere on the planet.

The interaction between attack and defence has always been present throughout history, from the basic fight between predator and prey to the unrelenting aggressiveness seen in wars between states. These two fundamental forces embody power, and their complex interactions determine how people, societies, and even whole civilizations will turn out.

While offence seems to have an unchallengeable hold on the situation, defence has exceptional potential and the intellectual prowess to make it a force to be reckoned with. We will examine the profound essence of attack and defence in this observant-philosophical investigation, analyse their functions, and discover the actual nature of power.

Attack: The Dominion of Aggression:

- In its purest form, an attack is a violent and aggressive act intended to overwhelm and enslave its target or foe. In order to establish dominance, it taps into the whole range of physical and mental power.
- Attack has consistently been manifested as a tool of power, from the predatory impulses of animals to the strategic military operations of governments.
- It has the attraction of having an instant effect since it takes the initiative and works to control how the

encounter is portrayed in the media.

In contrast, the actual measure of power is not just in the ability to strike, but also in the capacity to withstand.

Defence: The current endurance incumbent

- Defence stands out as the powerful defender of endurance in contrast to the seeming attraction of assault. It includes the array of defences, tactics, and brainpower that a person or entity uses to defend themselves from an adversary.
- Credibility and agility are essential for defence, which also calls for a thorough knowledge of one's weaknesses and the capacity to successfully mitigate them. It is a symbol of tenacity and unyielding survivalism.
- Defence fortifies one's position, enabling them to weather the storm and emerge resiliently, whereas assault aims to gain domination in the moment.

The strength of defence rests in its capacity for endurance,
which opens up several possibilities for counterattack and victory.

The Power contradiction:

- In the complex dance between assault and defence, a contradiction materialises, Attack's immediate effects and potential for conquest compel one to think of it as the personification of power. True power, on the other hand, transcends the use of physical force and comes to a head in the art of defence.

- Despite having great strength, the force that launches the attack ultimately prevails because it is able to withstand it. Defence sets the pace for supremacy with its intellectual power, creating chances and methods that shift the balance in its favour.

It is crucial to understand that any survivor, whether a predator or a country, has to be attacked in order to establish its existence. However, defence is what secures survival and makes it possible to pursue long-term objectives. In the natural world, predators must carry out successful hunts in order to survive, whereas their prey must use defence systems in order to survive and procreate. Similar to this, nations involved in conflicts need to have a strong defence to protect their sovereignty and development.

As a result, defence by its very nature becomes the determinant of survival and the basis for the pursuit of more ambitious goals.

> ***"The power may be in the attack's palm of the wrist,***
> ***but the defence is still able to take full advantage up until the second of choice."***

The African elephant is a magnificent illustration of the strength of defence in the animal kingdom. The African elephant is renowned for its calm disposition despite its enormous size and frightening power.

However, it exhibits a remarkable defensive reaction when confronted by predators like lions or hyenas.In the case of a predator encounter, African elephants will gather their herd and form a tight-knit protective circle around the young. The adult elephants will trumpet loudly and display their massive stature and long, curved tusks as a warning. They stop predators from attacking by erecting a strong wall of resistance.In this case, the African elephant's defence strategy is a perfect example of the advantages of collaboration, intelligence, and adaptability.

Elephants use their combined strength and their size as a deterrence to create an environment where the predator realises that an attack would be fruitless.

An example of how strength and intellect may be effective weapons for self-defense and maintaining the survival of the species is provided by the African elephant's defensive strategy.

Despite the fact that assault may seem to have the upper hand, defence draws its strength from the intellectual realm. Being able to anticipate, plan, and respond swiftly is the key to a successful defence.

The odds of the defender's survival are increased by their ability to seize opportunities and manipulate their surroundings.

It is the epitome of adaptation, allowing the defender to take advantage of the attacker's flaws, fend off aggressiveness, and come out on top. The human mind is capable of conjuring up incredible strategies and winning the war against overwhelming odds, therefore in this arena the power of defence transcends the flimsy force of assault.

In the never-ending struggle between offensive and defence, the true nature of power is revealed.

Attack may appear to be the immediate and powerful force,

while defence possesses inherent potential that extends

beyond straightforward violence.

Defence sets the parameters of conflict and determines the best course of action through its unwavering dedication, astute intellect, and robust might. It fosters adaptability, guarantees survival, and highlights the enormous potential of human brain.Our inner understanding gives us this strength, which enables the spirit of perseverance to triumph.

Why to hate ourselves

Like a volatile elixir, self-hatred poisons the self-worth reservoirs, destroying everything of one's identity in the process. One must build a bold path of self-compassion in order to travel this perilous terrain by releasing the thorny chains that bound the spirit.

Self-hatred serves as a sophisticated tool in the wide spheres of self-exploration, but the hidden fires of authenticity can only be rekindled by the recovery of self-love, kindling a bright tapestry of adaptation, development, and unconstrained fulfilment. It fits into every nook and cranny of the multidimensional cube that serves as a representation of who we are and allows us to explore the depths of our existence.

Only through self-hatred can we fully understand our qualities,

shortcomings, and ability for change.

In a culture with complex emotions and a wide range of opinions, the significance of understanding and honouring the functions of both love and hatred cannot be stressed.

This philosophical thesis embraces a youthful perspective that sees life with openness, curiosity, and a hunger for advancement in order to examine the power of these emotions, focusing in particular on the notion of hating hatred itself. We have seen the intricacy of both love and hatred in this philosophical examination.

When we detest hatred itself,
we become aware of the need of understanding and appreciating the subtleties of our emotions.

We want to create a society where love reigns supreme, encouraging personal growth, intellectual enlightenment, and harmonious coexistence.
We do this via introspection, cooperation, and a youthful perspective.

Why You're Worthless..!?

Are you truly deserving of this?

What really makes you WORTH.....?

Do you ever feel like you're worth something?

A basic truth that transcends age, media, and society standards may be found in the enormous fabric of human experience. In addition to being written in textbooks, pamphlets, and notice boards in public schools, this reality has also been whispered by the elderly and imprinted on brochures.

It is a truth that echoes down the passageways of time, encouraging us to accept the full measure of our worth and reject the cacophony of voices that want to devalue us out of envious vengeance.

Since the flame or consciousness spark that burns the very core of each of us is present within each of us. It is a flame that longs to blaze bright and exude the brilliance of our special life.

The whims of others or the constrained parameters of their vision do not determine our value. Instead, it is the expression of who we truly are, which is moulded by the decisions we make and the lives we lead.

It is simple to give in to the demands of conformity and to give in to the turbulent winds of societal expectations in a society full of judgements and comparisons. But we must keep in mind that our purpose in life goes beyond simply shaping ourselves into the wants of others.

> ***"We are here to forge our own paths,***
> ***to give life to the interests we hold dear,***
> ***and to sway to the beat of our own hearts."***

We are equipped with the means to mould our future, much like a skilled artisan. To carve out the delicate features of our dreams, we use the backsaw of our will. We stake our reputation on a firm position and refuse to bend to the whims of those who would minimise our goals. We don't have to wait for the vain approval of the fickle masses while we toil in the pursuit of what we love. Because the importance of our work lies not in what others may think, but in the act of creation itself.

We must embrace the endless possibilities that are available to us and reject the limitations of preconceived conceptions. The approval or denial of our requests shouldn't ever be used to judge our value because they are only one brief episode in the magnificent symphony of our life. I beg those who have struggled with uncertainty, who have questioned the purpose of their life, to understand that these are the echoes of a long-gone ghost.

The conviction that one is unworthy is a self-inflicted death, a mental prison from which one might be set free. As long as the spark of life continues to burn inside you, my dear reader, you have intrinsic value that cannot be destroyed.

However, among the diversity of mankind, there could be some who turn to mediocrity for consolation. They look at your colourful tapestry with envious eyes and use poisonous comments to try to bring down your spirits. But do not let their toxic chorus of jealousy affect you. Unless you give under their control, their words have no power over you.

You are in this fleeting existence to live a life that is honourable and deserving of the depth of your spirit. Accept the music of your passions, move to the beat of your aspirations, and allow the brilliance of your true self shine forth into the world.

In my utmost consideration,

"If any one of them are yelling out in WORTHLESS JEALOUSY
over your manner of life and living, you are WORTHLESS."

Fearing to, for and by FEAR

If I were to sum up this complex idea, I would say that it is the severe lack of contextual awareness that makes the existence of a sentient mind necessary. A vicious habit of disgust and anxiety takes root in the maze-like depths of ignorance, where most people inadvertently find themselves. Fear emerges, that mysterious force that captures the core of unadulterated emotion. It has no boundaries because individuals who lack cognitive aptitude or the ability to comprehend have an inbuilt potential for unrelenting horror. Surprisingly, it is the fools, the idiots, and the witless that get adulation because they have a remarkable talent for recognising exactly what they fear.

However, there is a segment of people within this broad tapestry of dread who shudder at the very notion of action taken without their approval or consideration. The danger that hides in the darkness rather than the darkness itself is what inspires terror. This fear, which is based on information gathered over a lifetime, is apprehension that results from the worry of being duped or mislead by unidentified entities.

Think back to the childlike fearlessness that is unencumbered by the weight of perception and blissfully unconcerned by the cryptic veil of darkness until the revelation of prospective hazards manifests itself. This realisation causes a feeling of dread and awakens the latent seeds of consciousness inside.

The word "conscious fear" accurately describes phobias, which are brought on by harmful encounters or the spread of unsettling information and cause panic to grasp the heart and horror to pervade one's entire being.

Our dread of perilous unknowns actually stems from the expanse of the unexplored. In this space of the unknown, apprehension grows like ivy and chokes our confidence to the very core. Since happy, fortunate occurrences by their very nature emanate excitement and delight, they don't appear to cause the heart to quiver at the mere thought of them. When trapped in the vice-like grip of anxiety and shrouded in the dense cloud of dread, joyous memories, however, disappear. The mind creates ominous images that amplify our dread of the unknown by weaving a negative tapestry based on a painful experience.

As a result, we are caught up in the willful phobia of the dark, an unsettling environment where dread and ignorance are intertwined. It is a philosophical riddle that calls us to go further into the depths of our awareness while testing the fundamental foundation of our understanding.

The study of dread takes on an intellectual dimension in this world of shadows as a quest to understand the complexities of human nature and the enormous effects of the unknown on our frail existence.

Everybody is a Nobody

"There was an important job to be done and
Everybody was sure that Somebody would do it.
Anybody could have done it, but Nobody did it.
Somebody got angry about that because it was
Everybody's job.
Everybody thought that Anybody could do it,
but Nobody realized that Everybody wouldn't do it.
It ended up that Everybody blamed Somebodywhen
Nobody did what Anybody could have done.
*- **Charles R. Swindoll**"*

Booooooooo...oooooo...oooooooo...ooooooooring

We get anxious, irritated, and frustrated when we are bored, the pernicious state of lifelessness that plagues our lives. Our cognitive processes become obsolete as a result of this disease, which is like a relentless algorithm that dumps them in the enormous mental junkyard. The crushing weight of ennui makes us realise how little we really are. Our brain withers, turning into a desolate wasteland devoid of meaning when we find ourselves imprisoned in its crushing grasp.

One must cut through the complex web of their own boredom in order to escape this deadly foe's grasp. When faced with subjective duties that go beyond simple self-preservation, the mind, which yearns for stimulation, comes to life. The cruellest forms of boredom highlight the darkest truths about life. When we choose inaction, it highlights the emptiness that permeates our spirits and amplifies the misery of being nothing.

Consequently, the issue of how to escape this constant grip of boredom emerges. It is conceivable since I have had the honour of conversing with a group of people who have pushed the boundaries of their own comfort zones through their distinctive techniques. In an effort to escape the grip of boredom, they have experimented with a wide range of actions and decisions. Out of all the possibilities, one idea jumps out: "Bored of being bored because being bored is boring."

However, there is an oasis in this barren terrain
for those who dare to create and for those who won't sit back and wait for things to happen.

"Boredom is an unfamiliar idea to the brilliant brains that create their own universe and give it meaning and purpose."

Anatomy of Monotony

Our innate curiosity and quest for knowledge are sewn deeply into the fabric of human existence.
However, despite this immense potential for development and fulfilment, we experience a paradoxical phenomenon—the eventual loss of deeply held passions.
There is a depressing loss of involvement and an overpowering sensation of weariness associated with this complicated disease, which is sometimes referred to as monotonous.

Numerous people's lives are ruled by monotony, which has an ensnaring hold over them and traps them in a web of disinterest. It all boils down to a basic conflict between our inborn need for novelty and the invasion of repetition and routine.

The human mind struggles against the restrictions of routine because it is always craving for novel experiences and intellectual stimulation. The novelty that once sparked enthusiasm fades into the background as familiarity becomes the norm, leaving an emptiness that resounds with disillusionment in its aftermath.

The stifling impact of cultural expectations is one potential reason for this decline in interest. People frequently become stuck in activities that fit in with society conventions but don't satisfy their actual inclinations. They unintentionally contribute to the depletion of motivation and the ensuing plunge into monotony by starting down a path devoid of personal significance because they are bound by the chains of responsibility.

The inherent joy people experience from their profession diminishes as they distance themselves from who they truly are, and as a result, they become disenchanted and disconnected.

In addition, the human psyche is a complicated patchwork of emotions, goals, and ambitions. The fires of passion can be extinguished if they are subjected to protracted periods of stress, exhaustion, or misfortune. The burden of obligations combined with the requirements of modern life may zap the very essence that previously ignited ardour and commitment. In such situations, people would experience indifference, which would make their passionate endeavours cumbersome and insignificant. Additionally, a lack of development and growth can lead to boredom. The need for both personal and professional growth drives people inherently.

The appeal of novelty wanes and boredom sets in when there is stagnation and a lack of difficulties.

The human soul, which is full of wonder and possibility, yearns for a life that is exciting and meaningful. Even the most impassioned individuals, though, can get trapped in the convoluted world of monotony. Understanding the anatomy of monotony allows us to untangle the complex threads that stifle our excitement and reveals a convergence of elements including cultural norms, emotional weariness, and stagnation.

Expectations drive life.

Expectations have a mixed reputation since they may lead to sadness and disappointment, but they can also be transforming forces that aid people in growing and becoming better versions of themselves. This makes them a dualistic concept because they arouse conflicting beliefs about their effects.

The combination of anticipation, reason, and emotion is a

complex and fascinating aspect of the human experience. While rational expectations are typically associated with better outcomes, emotional expectations can lead to disappointment and suffering. This philosophical research examines anticipation's dual nature and underlines how it functions effectively in reasoning but may pose challenges in emotion. We will use applicable examples, analogies, and quotations to help demonstrate the complexity of this phenomenon.

Understanding this range of possibilities is crucial because expectations may lead to either exceptional highs of achievement or catastrophic lows brought on by unmet expectations.

They are not only intangible ideas; they have the power to progress people. We may reach our full potential and assist others in realising theirs by comprehending the influence of expectations and using them to our benefit. Accepting expectations as a natural gift, gratifying our appetites, and moving forward on a path to self-awareness, growth, and fulfilment are all important steps to take.

The idea that "**Expectations do hurt you**" has pervaded human discourse for centuries is what we investigate in this discourse, along with expectations' nature, influence on human existence, and possibility for increasing our potential and attaining bigger things. I contend that the problem is not expectations per such, but rather our unique views and decisions.

In this inquiry, we look at how expectations significantly affect our lives. I argue that although having no expectations at all or very few expectations may lead to a life of boredom, embracing expectations allows us to live active and fulfilling lives.

By recognising the underlying risks and accepting the potential rewards, we may leverage the power of expectations to promote personal growth, modify our behaviours, and increase resilience.

Finding balance and controlling expectations are crucial for one's own wellbeing and a successful existence. Setting reasonable goals that are in line with our capacities and environmental conditions is the first step.

We may avoid the problems of having unreasonable expectations, which frequently result in disappointment and frustration, by being aware of our limitations and knowing what is feasible. Expectations may be difficult, but ultimately it is up to us how we respond to them. By accepting expectations, we may optimise our potential, modify our behaviours, and advance our personal growth. Instead of giving in to the aches expectations could cause, let's seize the opportunities they give.

By striking a delicate balance between ambition and satisfaction,
we may lead intriguing lives and make the most of the limited time we have to live.

But here comes the most important and interesting part of elements about 'EXPECTATION's,
it's the working nature,
EXPECTATIONS works powerful in rationality but Horribly fail with emotionally.

The working capacity of rational applications function well-performed than with the elements of logic and rationality that is because the structure of expectations are defined in imagination with relevant to the logic or rationally but at cases of emotional functioning it works horribly ill the causes cannot be more than thousands but possibly one and that is the expectations having more than one form.

For illustration, expecting a job with a potential view or working with a vision of achievement or reward does have a stable or significant requirements that help them to achieve like working well for the company with maintaining proper "working hour" attendance or getting imaginative which may assist the employer in the sense of HARD engaged force to simple working environment can be the vision of expectation that lead to an achievement or to regard of reward, but whereas in emotional function, these expectations are not stable or considerable and instead are based on a person's emotional.

For example, expecting a romantic partner to always understand and fulfill our emotional needs without communication or effort can lead to disappointment and hurt when reality falls short of these lofty expectations.

Rational expectations are built on logic and unbiased analysis. They require assessing the available data, drawing inferences based on the information, and forecasting outcomes that are accurate.

Expectations founded on logic and reason typically produce prudent decisions and favourable results.

"Expect the best, plan for the worst, and prepare to be surprised."

- Denis Waitley

In a business situation, it would be logical to assume that an entrepreneur would examine market trends, customer preferences, and financial projections before establishing goals and developing a plan of action. The chance of achieving the targeted outcomes rises as a result of this tactic.

Rational expectations serve as a compass that directs us on

a reasonable and calculated course towards the best interest of our goals when traversing uncertain terrain.

Emotional expectations are the offspring of desires, hopes, and arbitrary opinions. They include assuming what other people should do, think, or feel in light of our emotional needs or preferences. Emotional expectations may be influenced by personal preconceptions, fantasies, or idealised representations of others. But when these illogical or excessive expectations are not met, it typically leads to disappointment and hurt.

"Expectations were like fine pottery. The harder you held them, the more likely they were to crack."

- Brandon Sanderson

In a romantic relationship, emotional expectations for a partner could include anticipating unwavering adoration, flawless comprehension, and consistent support. Relationships may suffer, and individuals may feel distressed if these expectations aren't met.

They've been likened to flimsy glass castles constructed on ephemeral sands. Since they are constructed on unstable ground, they could fall apart if realism puts on display how fragile they are.

Rationality and emotion in balance: It's important to maintain a healthy balance between the two. Realistic expectations that are attuned to our wishes while still being based on reality are possible when we are able to recognise, comprehend, and balance our emotions with reason.

This harmony promotes emotional health, flexibility in judgement, and resilience.

The conflicting consequences that might result from both views are highlighted by the duality of expectation between reason and emotion. Although emotional expectations can result in disappointment and suffering, rational expectations offer a strong foundation for wise decision-making. Finding the balance between these two spheres gives us the ability to create more reasonable expectations, generate healthier relationships, and promote personal development.

We may successfully manage the complicated web of expectations by appreciating the strength of reason and the intricacy of emotions.

We are "FISH"y

As they are immersed by the fluidity of knowledge, humans resemble fish in the vast ocean of existence. The question of whether these aquatic creatures are conscious of the aquatic environment in which they dwell does arise, though. Our ability to successfully navigate the challenges of life is made possible by knowledge, which assumes the divine form of wisdom. But it is distressing to observe how many individuals, in the midst of their journey, find solace in declaring,

"This limited knowledge is all I possess," or, worse still, display a reluctance to embrace new information. These claims only serve to demonstrate how dumb they are. Albert Einstein, a famous figure in intellectual dialogue, left us with a timeless proverb that reads,

"Two things are infinite: the universe and human stupidity; and I'm not sure about the universe."

These insightful remarks hold up a mirror to the condition of the human race despite possessing a tinge of wit. The dreadful inclination of humans to willfully limit their mental faculties by enclosing themselves in the confines of ignorance is brought to light by them. I genuinely feel conflicted when I see folks like these—a tinge of pity coupled with the tiniest smile on my lips.

You should feel sorry for them because of their own intellectual decay, which amounted to rejecting their existence as anything other than physical beings and dissipating the vast knowledge reserves that were waiting for them.

Nevertheless, I can't help but giggle a little since these individuals accidentally brand themselves as dumb propagandists by becoming the personification of their own stupidity.

RIGHT and WRONG are never RIGHT and WRONG.

GOOD and BAD are never GOOD and BAD.....

We have been trained to view the world through the prism of good and bad, positives and negatives, from the earliest phases of human development. But philosophy has always sought to understand the underlying essence of what makes anything good or bad, positive or negative, and right or wrong. We will examine the intricacies of these ideas in this article, as well as how our knowledge of them is shaped by our own experiences, society conventions, and individual viewpoints. We shall make an effort to peel back the many layers that characterise these essential facets of human existence via a philosophical perspective. Discussions about morals and ethics are difficult simply because of language barriers. The multifaceted nature of human experiences and ethical decision-making is difficult to describe using terms like good, bad, positive, negative, right, and wrong.

Although language is a useful tool, it can never adequately express the complexity of moral conceptions. Knowing that language has its limits inspires us to approach moral debates with humility and a willingness to engage in complex conversation.

The concepts of good and bad are intricately linked to human viewpoints and preferences. What one person deems to be good may not always be the same for another. Our understanding of what is good is frequently driven by our desire for our own comfort and well-being, but it is important to understand that this does not imply a standard that is relevant to all people. Determining what is good and wrong is a difficult task with many facets.

These ideas are strongly impacted by societal, cultural, and personal belief systems. What is perceived as right in one group could be judged incorrect in another. Setting up objective moral standards is difficult since good and wrong are subjective concepts. Additionally, the pursuit of right and wrong is an ongoing process, with each conclusion posing fresh questions. Philosophers have debated ethical ideas and principles for centuries since there are no generally recognised definitions or categories of morality.

*Being **good** is about making choices that avoid harm and help those in need;*
it cannot be reduced to a simplistic image of perfection or compassion.

Since there are multiple ways to see the outcomes of our actions, there are several interpretations and evaluations of what is beneficial and detrimental.

Positive thinking, the desire to grow individually,
and an openness to taking lessons
from experiences are commonly associated with positivity.
Negativity, on the other side,
is frequently regarded as having
a pessimistic outlook and expecting the worst.

Positive and **Negative** attitudes are usually linked to optimistic and pessimistic mindsets, respectively.

However, it's important to distinguish between toxic negativity and the flaws that support negative opinions. It is better to avoid negative people since they can be going through despair, worry, or challenging circumstances in their lives.

The spread of knowledge and the development of a more compassionate society are both facilitated by helping persons who are depressed and demonstrating empathy for them. It is critical to remember that negative attitudes and feelings may be caused by underlying problems like depression, anxiety, or difficult living conditions. It might be inappropriate to judge someone adversely without taking into account their shortcomings or difficulties

It is frequently more beneficial to provide assistance and understanding to negative individuals as opposed to ignoring them, taking into account the possibility that their negativity may be a result of their own struggles. Discussions of good and evil, positive and negative, and right and wrong frequently exhibit binary thinking. Such dualistic methods, meanwhile, oversimplify the complex complexities of moral judgement. Human behaviour is a continuum, and categorising it into narrow groups limits our ability to comprehend the nuances involved in moral decisions. Understanding the many shades of grey enables a more thorough and considerate investigation of moral quandaries.

Our sense of good and evil, positive and negative, and right and wrong is significantly shaped by our perspective. By looking at these ideas from many angles, we may develop empathy and widen our minds. Our views are influenced by the situation in which an activity takes place, the motives driving it, and any possible outcomes. When analysing ethical decisions, having an open mind is encouraged by acknowledging this subjectivity.

The concepts of good and evil, positive and negative, and right and wrong, which have an impact on our perceptions and behaviour, profoundly affect human consciousness. They are, nevertheless, susceptible to human interpretation, cultural influences, and life experiences due to their inherent complexity and variety.

The intricacy of these concepts requires intellectual humility and a desire to participate in philosophical reflection. By understanding the nuances and ambiguities surrounding these notions, we may be able to cultivate a more compassionate and sensitive attitude when navigating the moral terrains of our lives.

By examining good and horrible, positive and negative, and right and wrong, we may see the depth and diversity of these notions. Subjectivity, perspective, and linguistic limitations all contribute to the complexity of moral decision-making.

To accept this complexity, one must let go of binary thinking and have a desire to engage in thoughtful observation and dialogue. By improving our understanding of these concepts, we may build a more compassionate and empathic society that honours the different perspectives that shape our moral landscape.

Conflicting Decisions and Battle of Thought Processes

Within the depths of our consciousness, there is a continual fight between our thoughts and our decision-making procedures. This philosophical theory makes an effort to explore the complexity of this conflict by shedding light on the variables that influence our decisions and the ways in which they are influenced by outside variables and other points of view.

> ***"Individuals frequently struggle to successfully navigate their lives and confidently make important decisions because of the hesitations and concerns that result from this internal conflict."***

The essence of the internal conflict is a contradiction between what one knows and what one feels. This tension, which results from the collision of emotional responses and cognitive awareness, gives rise to conflicting notions and uncertainty. The human mind is an intricate tapestry in which every experience, fact, and feeling are delicately woven with one another. While making a decision, these elements may pull in many directions, which would be upsetting.

Knowledge serves as a basis for decision-making and is gained via education, experience, and observation. It provides a clear foundation for comprehending the world's total complexity. But the emotional world adds richness and depth to our experiences. Emotions are emotive, illogical feelings that affect the way we perceive the world and frequently trump reason.

There is a dissonance created when these two worlds interact,
and this creates the conditions for internal conflict.

Anxiety is frequently the root of interpersonal conflicts. The root of these behaviour is our basic desire for security and self-preservation. The human species has evolved a strong inclination for caution and foresight as a result of intensive social indoctrination. These ingrained concerns in us provide us comfort despite their fundamentally unsettling nature.

Anxiety, ironically, makes us feel safe since it keeps us alert and ready for any dangers. The ramifications of this elevated anxiety. In contrast, might have both positive and negative effects. Even our anxieties, which have historically worked to keep us safe, might unexpectedly act against us. They could seem as an intense aversion to taking chances or as a paralysing resistance to change.

Ambivalence is not only a simple binary opposition; it can also take the form of a number of conflicting opinions, sentiments, and reactions to a certain topic, situation, or object. Due to their various features and the complexities that go along with them, our identities are complicated. It is essential to accept and understand this complexity in order to sort through the internal conflicts.

Making decisions is frequently clouded by mistakes made in the past and potential repercussions, which complicates the internal conflict further. Strong feelings like regret, remorse, and anxiety can render people helpless and prevent them from taking chances or committing to choices. The uncertainty of the future or the dread of making the same mistakes again can cloud rational thought and obstruct development. The pressure on people to make the "right" decisions may also be increased by societal and cultural expectations.

The conflict between one's knowledge and one's emotions is intensified by this external aspect, which feeds the internal struggle even more.

To find comfort from the internal conflict, people must go on a journey of introspection and self-discovery. Recognising the fundamental issues that feed a dispute is the first step in trying to resolve it. People can make deliberate decisions by being more self-aware because they may become aware of their preconceptions, anxieties, and opposing points of view.

Accepting uncertainty and the reality that mistakes are unavoidable helps people break free from the bonds of hesitation.

We must go on a journey of self-discovery and self-empowerment in order to escape the limitations imposed by the internal struggle. We must address our worries and anxieties head-on if we are to comprehend the complexity of our thoughts and emotions. We get insight into the reasons behind our divergent viewpoints and begin to sever the web of links that bind us as a result of this process. By increasing self-awareness and boosting self-confidence, we may overcome the limitations of indecision and embrace a life that is marked by fulfilment and significance.

When people take the time to think back on their previous mistakes and reframe setbacks as opportunities for progress, they are better equipped to go forward with confidence.

A person's comprehension of the world may also be expanded by seeking out opposing viewpoints and participating in open debate, and firmly held ideas may be challenged. People may transcend the confines of their own viewpoints and handle the complexity of decision-making with more clarity by encouraging intellectual humility and empathy.

One of the fundamental aspects of the human experience is the conflict that exists inside us between our cognitive and decision-making processes. It is a struggle that goes on in the background of our brains, driven by worries, opposing viewpoints, mistakes made in the past, and potential repercussions. To find a solution and clear the way for confident decision-making, it is important to comprehend and be aware of these elements.

A fundamentally human conflict that penetrates our life is the battle going on inside our heads between thinking and action. We all struggle with competing ideas, worries, and external influences that make it difficult for us to make decisions that are both logical and firmly held.

The secret to our liberty rests in the depths of our internal conflict between our intellect and decision-making processes.

We may overcome the constraints of uncertainty and anxiety by using the strength of self-reflection, insight, and self-confidence.

We may live lives of profound purpose,
limitless fulfilment,
and the power to control our own destinies by accepting our genuine selves and paving our own paths.

By embracing self-reflection, self-awareness, and a willingness to challenge our own biases, we can begin to untangle the knots of internal conflicts. It is through this journey that we can learn to embrace uncertainty, make peace with past mistakes, and navigate the complexities of decision-making with greater confidence and purpose.

In the realm of the internal war, it is in self-power to find harmony and transcend the limitations that hinder self growth and fulfillment.

"ESCAPE"ISM

Escapism has always been stigmatised by society as a bad trait or imperfection in human nature.
But if we change the way we look at things,
we may see that escapism is a worldview that is inherently human.

We will examine the idea of escapism in this philosophical theory and make the case that it is an essential component of human existence that promotes wellbeing, creativity, and personal development.
We may strike a delicate balance between facing obstacles and embracing the transformational potential of imaginative inquiry by acknowledging escapism as a natural urge.

The nature of escapism: At its foundation, escapism is a natural reaction to life's difficulties and complexity. It results from the need to briefly remove oneself from the taxing elements of reality.

Reading, creating art, listening to music, daydreaming, and even walking outside have all been ways that humans have historically sought relief from their concerns. These attempts to flee serve as a catalyst for relaxation, reflection, and regeneration.

Human imagination has a strong connection between creativity and escape. Through imagination, we construct new worlds, explore unexplored territory, and consider options that transcend the limitations of our present environment. Escapism helps individuals to depart from conventional thought processes, which fosters innovation and the expansion of creativity.

By taking innovative vacations,
we may be receptive to new ideas and perspectives,
which advances both our own development and that of society.

Escapism is used by the brain as a coping strategy, providing momentary reprieve from stress, anxiety, and other emotional problems. Reading engrossing books or watching engrossing films, among other hobbies that take us to other worlds, provide our minds a much-needed rest. Our general well-being is eventually improved since it enables us to refuel and recover emotional balance.

Escapism is crucial for fostering empathy and understanding as well as giving us the opportunity to contemplate, take care of ourselves, and recuperate emotionally. Through narratives and storytelling, escapism enables individuals to put themselves in the shoes of characters with a range of backgrounds and experiences. By empathising with these hypothetical or imagined characters, we broaden our perspectives, face biases, and develop a greater regard for the diversity of human existence. In this sense, escapism fosters social cohesion and empathy for others.

Escapism has many advantages, but it's important to find a balance between it and facing obstacles. Avoiding problems all the time might hinder personal growth and prolong a downward spiral towards escapism. Escapism, however, may provide people the mental respite they require to address their problems with new vigour and creativity if used carefully.

- **Humans require timesof rest and recharge** identical to the creatures that hibernate throughout the winter. We may save energy and meet obstacles with renewed energy by taking pauses and briefly withdrawing from daily obligations.

- **Seeking Better Opportunities**: Humans frequently look for change and new experiences in order to develop and flourish, much like birds that migrate to new areas in search of better habitats. Success and personal growth can result from getting out of bad conditions and looking into new chances.
- **Breaking for Safety**: Much as how animals disguise themselves to be safe, we may employ escapism to keep ourselves safe. We can briefly protect ourselves from stress and difficulties by partaking of acts that offer mental rest.
- **Personal Growth and Transformation**: Just like a caterpillar turning into a butterfly, escapism can result in personal development. Life may alter dramatically when we take the time to think on our actions and engage in creative pursuits.
- **Exploration of the Imagination**: Adults can also benefit from occasional periods of escape, just like children do. We get fresh perspectives and social abilities by exploring our imagination and creativity through hobbies, leisure, or daydreaming.

We develop problem-solving abilities and new views by embracing escapism. Society ought to see it favourably rather than negatively. By appreciating its significance, we can build a society that is caring. Schools and communities should promote healthy escapism to foster imagination and wellbeing. When viewed as a natural mentality, getting away has many positive effects on both people and society as a whole. It cultivates empathy, fosters creativity, supports psychological well-being, and fosters imagination.

We may live more fully and richly by enjoying escapism and finding a healthy balance with overcoming obstacles. It's time to recognise escapism as a fundamental aspect of the human experience that promotes individual development and societal understanding.

Intensity

A person's capacity to work productively and accomplish their goals is significantly influenced by their intensity, both in terms of personal drive and emotional depth. It includes one's behaviour strength, dedication, effort, assertiveness, and attentional concentration. When a person's passion is at its peak, it may be so strong that it can even outperform the most addictive substances in terms of elevating one's sense of fulfilment and purpose.

The tremendous influence of intensity on learning, personal development, and
the decisions we make in the quest of knowledge is explored in this philosophical insight.

- ***The Relationship Between Learning and Intensity:*** At its foundation, intensity is a very individual and individualised experience. It moves beyond the realm of simple emotions and develops into a deliberate action—an active induction point—that propels people to fervently pursue their passions.
  We get significance and depth from our environment by exerting intensity, which reveals layers of information and comprehension behind the apparent realities.
- **Intense** enthusiasm may be a learning catalyst since it motivates people to learn more and go deeper into a subject. We reach a level of increased attention,

dedication, and effort when we tackle a subject or field with unshakable intensity.

Due to this intensity, we are compelled to examine every detail and reveal subtleties and intricate details that could have gone missed otherwise. We are driven to continue learning and improve personally by the great enthusiasm we pursue.

- ***Choosing Intensity***: A Personal Journey: In a world filled with myriad choices and distractions, the decision to embrace intensity becomes a defining aspect of personal growth. Every individual has the power to choose their level of intensity in pursuing knowledge. For some, every pursuit, no matter how trivial, becomes an intense quest for understanding.
- But it's crucial to recognise that not all passions will arouse the same degree of fervour. While some projects may have a profound impact, others could only be preferences or fleeting fancies.

We can tell the difference between genuine passion and mere tendency via discernment and self-awareness.

- ***The Illusion of Intensity***: There are several levels of depth and passion within the area of intensity. The discovery implies that actual intensity can only be found at the extremes of the spectrum—either the peak of emotion or its absence.

Even when it seems passionate, the gap in between can just be a facade—a like rather than a strong desire. Individuals may manage their activities more skillfully by focusing their efforts on the truly challenging tasks by being aware of this distinction.

- **A Lifelong Journey Towards Intensity:** Intensity is a lifelong journey towards learning and personal development. Continuous self-reflection, introspection, and a readiness to accept the difficulties that come with passionate endeavours are necessary.

People may develop intensity as a motivating factor in their life by being committed and persistent, overcoming cultural norms and creating their own particular route to knowledge and self-fulfillment.

Random quotes phrases/Expressions that fuel up to think about Intensity more Intensly

- **"Intense passion is the fuel that ignites the fire of learning and propels us towards boundless knowledge."**
- "In the realm of intensity, every pursuit is an opportunity to suckle from the breasts of chance, nourishing our thirst for wisdom."
- **"Intensity is the compass that guides us through the maze of life, urging us to choose the path of relentless pursuit and discovery."**
- "True intensity surpasses the allure of the ephemeral, offering a higher high than any substance can provide."
- **"Within the depths of intensity lies the transformative power to transcend the ordinary and uncover extraordinary insights."**

It is impossible to overstate the transforming effect of intensity as a motivating factor in the search for knowledge.

People only learn more deeply, experience personal growth, and start a lifelong learning path when they are intense. By deciding to be intense, we defy social expectations and embrace the entire range of our interests. We really flourish and find fulfilment in this environment of extreme concentration, making the most of our time and feelings in the never-ending search for knowledge.

Everyone are BORN wonderful

Every living creature possesses unique traits, yet external factors usually obstruct self-awareness or distort perception. Success in life depends on being aware of, understanding, and successfully utilising each of our individual skills.

Time and emotions are our most valuable resources, yet they are also fleeting. The discovery raises a serious issue: cultural influences on people frequently limit their genuine skills, making them appear common or even "dumb."

The incredible potential that each individual possesses may be stifled by social expectations, constrained beliefs, and the need to fit in. In order for people to escape the constraints of society conventions and embrace their intrinsic magnificence, it is necessary to fight these conditioning influences. Our most important resources are time and emotions, but they pass quickly.

The only way we can make the best use of our time and feelings is to keep an undistorted viewpoint.

Even while each living thing has distinctive skills and characteristics, external influences can interfere with self-awareness or skew perceptions. Whether it is the deer's speed, the lion's ferocious scream, the eagle's soaring flight, or the depths of knowledge and beauty, every individual is blessed with a unique potential. But societal constraints, cultural norms, and upbringing frequently limit people's capacity to fully embrace and express their intrinsic genius. This philosophical investigation aims to elucidate the notion that everyone is an incredible human being with wonderful traits at their core, despite cultural conditioning that would lead one to believe otherwise.

Every person has unique qualities that set them apart from the rest of humanity's vast diversity. We need to be aware of who we are in order to act appropriately and prevent wasting these precious resources. To do this, we must free ourselves from the influence of religion, cultural norms, and the error of attributing our situation to fate or the deeds of others.I never linked my success to a specific attitude; rather, I believed it resulted from my readiness to accept the consequences of my decisions. It's true that I made a lot of bad choices—the majority of them, in fact. However, I will always remember the intense exhilaration I had while on the journey. This cycle of decisions and pleasure shapes my existence; it has taken on a life of its own and has become the very core of who I am.

There are thousands more amazing people who are just waiting to realise their full potential, including the great cook, athletic prodigy, smart person, and mathematical genius. It is crucial to know that everyone possesses intelligence and skills that are inherent to them just by virtue of their being. But they frequently have their ideas shaped by their upbringing, societal expectations, and cultural standards, which keeps them from realising their full potential.

To release the enormous potential that lives inside each and every person, it is essential to create an atmosphere that encourages individuality and allows individuals the opportunity to freely follow their interests and talents. We can create a culture that embraces diversity and promotes personal growth by encouraging individuals to explore their abilities and passions. By focusing on the inherent worth of each person's genius, we help people realise their full potential and share their special talents with the world.

Each person gains when their awesomeness is acknowledged and celebrated, and it also improves the quality of life for all others. In society, there are many different abilities and traits that may be appreciated and supported. By doing so, we can encourage creativity, teamwork, and mutual progress. A tremendous synergy that advances mankind is created when we cultivate a culture that honours each person's unique talents.

We must rethink what greatness is and question conventional ideas of success if we are to embrace the idea that everyone is an extraordinary individual. It urges a change in mentality that places social demands behind personal fulfilment, personal development, and the pursuit of hobbies. We create a culture that recognises each person's unique journey and gives them the freedom to realise their full potential and have a good effect on the world by giving individuals the freedom to pick their own paths.

Waiting for assistance and permission before taking any action, whether it be an action taken as a consequence of a choice or decision, or in the least worst case, thinking, has always been the most definitive and ultimate method to prove that you are an idiot.

One must be highly conscious of his own credibility and mental process, as well as the nature of its structure, in order to be a perfect, contented, and delightful guy for oneself. The ultimate level of self-helplessness a person can achieve is waiting to become the man or woman they once dreamed of being, which initially deters other people from offering to assist them.

Hallucination of Hard-work

The idea of hard labour has been elevated as the essential component for success in the world of human endeavours. We uncover a paradox that lies at the heart of this concept, though, when we go more into the framework of it.

This philosophical investigation seeks to illuminate the complex interconnections between desire, purpose, choice, and the search for fulfilment. We set out on a mission to identify the real road to a meaningful living by drawing motivation from the words of people who had battled false passions and societal pressures.

On our journey through life, we encounter countless individuals who, inspired by forces outside of themselves, take part in pursuits that have little or nothing to do with their core objectives. These false cravings, which are like passing mirages in the desert, lead us astray.

Instead of the effort put out, what bothers me is the lack of true passion for the subject at hand. In certain situations, one must listen to that voice since the heart and intellect possess an innate wisdom that cannot be suppressed.Hard effort done in the absence of true love is like to starving a rose of water and sunlight. It may seem lively on the outside, but the vibrancy and fragrance that come from being rooted in one's genuine purpose are absent, leaving its essence to fade away. No matter how attentively one takes care of it, a rose can never completely bloom if it is not given the sustenance of true desire

"Passion, without purpose, is a flame destined to burn out in darkness."
Kahlil Gibran,

Each person is born with a special purpose and a responsibility that must be carried out. The heart and intellect desire to harmonise with this goal because they are sensitive to the cosmic symphony of reality. Going off this route and into unfamiliar territory is quite taxing on the soul. We develop a variety of illnesses that no amount of medicine can cure when we give up on our genuine calling.

The body, the container of our existence, yearns for harmony with our true calling, a dance in which satisfaction emerges as the supreme song. The ability to make decisions is within the sphere of human agency. We make our way through life's maze by making consciously thought-out decisions. Although striving for achievement and fulfilment is admirable, hard effort is not the only factor.

Success is elusive, like the mystifying chameleon, and is not determined by appearances or tangible wealth.
There is no absolute state for Success to exist-in, the decisions we make shape the way to where we're going, and they contain the intangible core of great success.

"Do not go where the path may lead, go instead where there is no path and leave a trail."
Ralph Waldo Emerson

Society, which is constantly the source of expectations, perpetuates the fallacy that intelligence or success are tied to outward symbols. A beautiful home or a high-end car are examples of visible prosperity, but knowledge and satisfaction are not necessarily brought on by their mere existence. Your obligations, kinship relations, family, etc. But if you want to assist and care for them, you are behaving in accordance with your wishes.

The majority of people, whether they are compelled by others or themselves,

behave and do acts out of habit rather than out of a sincere wish to do so.

"He who knows that enough is enough will always have enough."
Sage Lao Tzu

We frequently become trapped in a never-ending loop of pursuing empty aspirations in our chase of these transient markers. Understanding that one's character development and pursuit of real passions are the true measures of success is the mark of true wisdom.

Hard labour is a symbol of the human spirit's tenacity and will in the magnificent fabric of existence. To embrace the power of true passion and purpose, one must, however, rise beyond the constrictions of cultural expectations.

It's crucial to distinguish between actively working on something you might not love and ostensibly being enthusiastic.Think of your efforts as a shaky bridge that you have to cross across a valley of unmet expectations. Like a powerful wind, society and peer pressure force people to walk on this deteriorating structure. The weight of their sincere goals and aspirations is ebbing away with each step, trapping them in a state of misery as they move. Even if societal or peer pressure may occasionally lead people to make professional decisions that are at odds with their true preferences, this doesn't necessarily suggest that their efforts were in vain. Even yet, there is still a chance that it will lead to useful interactions, personal growth, and even chance meetings.

But if someone constantly works on things they don't like or aren't interested in,

it can cause discontent and have a detrimental impact on their mental and physical health.

We must pay attention to our hearts' nudges and use conscious decision-making as a weapon on the long path to fulfilment. Only then is it possible to break free from the bonds of false desires, reveal our genuine path, and open the door to a life rich in significance, profundity, and fulfilment.

Success in the symphony of existence is not just the result of hard work, but also the harmonic interaction of one's honesty, purpose, and decisions made along the road.

Mentality of Multiple personalities

The human mind is a sophisticated and intricate area capable of showing a broad range of emotions and behaviour that may look inconsistent or bizarre. The phenomena of many identities, also known as dissociative identity disorder, sheds light on the perplexing nature of our mental environment.

This philosophical theory attempts to study the behavioural components and underlying emotional causes that give rise to the appearance of many personalities inside an individual, resulting in a variety of distinct and oftentimes perplexing behaviour.

This theory is based on the understanding that people are complex beings with a wide range of feelings, ideas, and experiences. Each individual is a mosaic of memories, convictions, and aspirations that come together to create their own personality. This sense of self is dynamic and sensitive to the ups and downs of life's events, though; it is not static. Our emotions and mental health alter throughout the day, much like the tide and the wind, giving rise to many facets of our personalities.

I discover that there are many different people and points of view when I explore the world of my own emotions. I see a change in my opinions and responses, regardless of whether I am working, eating, yelling, or absorbed in a movie.

I find it fascinating to read articles that look at psychological studies and surveys that look at how people could act differently depending on their emotional states. When their emotions are at their highest, even someone who is normally calm might become irritable and prone to anger.

Multiple personality disorder has an intriguing and mysterious element due to how difficult it is to fathom how it operates. While some people who seek therapy discover that their experiences are classified as unique personalities, I believe that the phenomena of feeling a spectrum of emotions is more frequent than we realise.

The appearance of multiple personalities is also influenced by the milieu in which a person finds themselves. Specific reactions may be elicited by certain persons, circumstances, or stimuli, leading to a change in behaviour or perspective.

For example, a person could be reserved and quiet in one setting but become animated and happy with close friends or when working on a passion project. These changes illustrate the dynamic nature of human psychology as well as the enormous effect that external factors have on our internal experience. I often choose to be silent and watch during crucial times in my personal path. But occasionally, especially when I'm taking part in a screening of my beloved movie, I experience feelings that are too intense. A scene or a character may be elevated and become heroes thanks to an inventive fusion of technical elements and an engaging narrative.

This heightened emotional state may also show at times of hunger, when my senses become more acute, or when I meet someone with an equally quirky mentality, which sparks a talkative side in me.

Emotional triggers have a significant role in the emergence of multiple personas. When faced with intense emotions like anger, joy, grief, or fear, our minds may adapt and respond in a variety of ways. During these moments, some aspects of our personality may come to the fore while others may become more repressed. The combination of emotions and personality traits leads to our experience of several personas, each of which reflects a distinct aspect of who we are.

Recognising the adaptability of emotions and how they affect our opinions and actions is fascinating. Finding and examining these many personalities inside ourselves may help us better understand our own complexity as well as the wide range of human experience, even though it can be perplexing at times. The complexity and fluidity of the human mind are demonstrated by many personalities' mentalities.

Understanding the effects of feelings, environmental factors, and personal experiences can help us better understand the broad range of behaviour and points of view that people exhibit. Accepting the coexistence of many personalities in both ourselves and others can help us develop compassion, acceptance, and a deeper appreciation of the exquisite intricacy of human existence. It serves as a reminder that rather than being limited to a particular way of being, we have the ability for a range of dynamic emotional landscapes.

Crime I look at....

In essence, society serves as a lens through which to define crime.

Since the beginning of time, crime has been a topic of moral and ethical assessment, with society frequently classifying it as either good or evil, right or wrong. A wide-ranging phenomena, crime has origins in many parts of human life. It is the result of a number of interrelated circumstances, with vengeance and money acting as its primary drivers.

Additionally, there is a symbiotic relationship between crime and society since social norms influence how crime is defined and social tensions influence how crime occurs. We acquire understanding of the complicated interrelationship between crime, society, and the underlying forces that motivate people to violate the law by exploring these complexity.

The French Resistance, an underground movement that emerged during World War II, undertook a range of activities that were deemed criminal by the occupying Nazi forces. These activities included acts of sabotage, espionage, and smuggling, which were carried out with the explicit intention of resisting the oppressive occupation and safeguarding the freedom and survival of their nation.

While the actions of the French Resistance were illegal and classified as crimes under the occupation, their motivation stemmed from a deep-rooted desire to protect the values and principles that defined their country. Their acts of defiance were driven by a strong sense of duty towards their fellow citizens and an unwavering commitment to preserving the fundamental rights and dignity of the French people.

In the face of immense adversity, the members of the French Resistance saw their criminal activities as a necessary means to resist the occupying forces, disrupt their operations, and provide vital support to those persecuted or oppressed. Their bravery and sacrifice continue to be celebrated as a testament to the indomitable spirit of those who stood up against injustice, fighting for the survival and liberation of their nation.

The French Resistance serves as a powerful example of how individuals, driven by a higher purpose, can defy conventional laws and engage in what may be classified as criminal activities to uphold principles of freedom, justice, and human rights.

Mafia groups and drug cartels are two prominent examples of organised criminal syndicates. These organisations participate in a variety of illegal activities, including as the trafficking of illegal substances, extortion, and violent crimes.

Their main goal is to maximise their personal financial benefit, frequently at the expense of the welfare of defenceless people and whole communities. These criminal organisations prioritise their own interests above moral concerns in their never-ending quest for power and riches. As a result of sustaining a cycle of societal unhappiness, they weaken the basis of law and order. Their actions not only foster a culture of fear and insecurity but also contribute to the moral principles of society being lost.

To go above these simplistic binary classifications and appreciate the complex nature of crime, the underlying reasons of criminal activity must be investigated. By focusing on the consequences that affect criminal activity, we may be able to gain a more nuanced understanding of crime and its role in society. This philosophical theory attempts to comprehend crime by looking at it through the lens of its consequences and taking into consideration the many diverse factors that affect it.

If society views an action as consistent with its ideals, then it is not a crime at all. An action is not illegal until society proclaims. it to be such. Crime is an act that disobeys society's rules and puts it in risk, hence it has to be punished. We must take into account the social, economic, and psychological factors that affect a person's behaviour in order to understand crime.

Crime is not a solitary occurrence; rather, it is a reflection of a larger socio-cultural context.

Criminal behaviour is frequently a reaction to perceived or actual injustices. Marginalisation, poverty, inequality, and a lack of chances can all have an impact on the sense of pessimism or despair that drives people to commit crimes. Similar to how a broken mirror exposes how divided society is, crime may serve as a mirror that reveals a community's flaws and vulnerabilities. By understanding the origins and repercussions of crime, society's shattered parts may be pieced back together, and efforts may be taken to establish a more secure and tranquil atmosphere.

These fundamental reasons must be understood in order to understand the results that motivate criminal behaviour.

It's critical to understand that every illegal conduct is motivated by factors other than monetary gain or self-gratification. Criminal behaviour is typically motivated by mental anguish, extreme suffering, or a desire for vengeance. It is necessary for society attitudes towards offenders to change in order to implement a strategy that concentrates on comprehending the effects of crime.

The main priorities should be empathy, rehabilitation, and social reintegration rather than punishment alone. Using crime as a teaching tool can help society develop empathy and compassion. By examining the effects of criminal behaviour, one can gain a better understanding of what drives individuals to commit crimes.

It could be able to focus efforts on the key problems and offer the right help and resources by being aware of the causes and consequences that contributed to criminal behaviour. The social environment can help break the cycle of crime and its consequences by promoting social cohesiveness and aiding in rehabilitation.

When criminals feel oppressed or marginalised by society's norms or institutions, they may perceive their activities as a way to reclaim power or pursue justice. Understanding the root causes of these effects may help us better comprehend the intricate linkages that exist between criminal conduct, social pressures, and individual experiences.

The primary goal of laws is to penalise criminal behaviour, and society's desire to curtail criminal activity served as the impetus for the creation of these laws. In order to comprehend it, one needs to look at the historical perception of witchcraft as something that was forbidden and subject to punishment.

The laws created to stop it are greatly influenced by how society defines crime.

Society's opinion on the particular activity is important for defining crime because, for example, if society does not consider giving bribes to be crimes, they will not be recorded as such and no laws will be imposed on them even though they are morally wrong.

In addition to the direct impacts it has on people engaged, crime also has greater implications on society as a whole. We can evaluate how crime impacts victims, communities, and the criminal justice system, among other stakeholders, by being aware of its repercussions. By examining the consequences of crime, we may identify patterns, weak points, and systemic problems that contribute to its perpetuation. Since crime has so many different causes and outcomes, it is hard to describe it as either good or evil or right or wrong due to its complexity. By adopting a philosophical framework that sees crime through the lens of consequences, we may better comprehend the fundamental dynamics of crime.

"My World": A Realm of Subjectivity and Inner Reflection

Within the vast fabric of existence, each individual lives in a unique world filled with thoughts, emotions, and opinions that shape their experience. This inner world, which is different from the outer world, acts as a refuge where one's personal beliefs and interests are allowed to dominate without interference from other forces.

We examine the concept of "My World" as a place of subjectivity, introspection, and the enormous impact it may have on our lives in this philosophical research.

Like an ocean, our inner world is vast and teeming with life. Each wave in the song "My World" represents the ebb and flow of our thoughts, feelings, and desires, and each wave contains the essence of who we are.

In "My World," the limits of perception extend beyond what can be physically felt. It is a world where, as they are depicted on our mental canvas, thoughts and ideas rule supreme. In this area, our own perspective on the world becomes the main tool for interpretation. Unrestricted by the viewpoints of others, our own perspectives and interests become the guiding factors that define our sense of reality.

Emotions and sentiments also constitute the fundamental essence of our lives. They are hidden in the recesses of our minds, at the very centre of who we are. These emotions, which are intricately related to our ideas, exert a powerful impact on our perceptions, decisions, and choices, which in turn shapes our experiences. Our inner emotional landscape significantly influences the results we want and the directions we choose as we move through the world.

"My World" recognises that each person's world is essentially unique and embraces the strength of uniqueness. It accepts the notion that no two people view the world or experience it in the same way. Personal values, beliefs, and wants blend together in this subjective space to create a tapestry that is particular to each person.

It serves as a reminder that, despite our differences, all of our viewpoints are legitimate and deserving of respect. It is a monument to the diversity and depth of human existence.

Expectations from the outside world don't really matter in "My World."

It frees us from the burden of having to live up to social expectations or other people's standards. Here, internal

affirmation is subordinate to authenticity and self-expression.
It is a place where we are unrestricted in our ability to investigate, query, and reevaluate how we perceive the world, acting only on the basis of our inner compass and the themes that speak to us deeply.

Fantasy and ingenuity abound in "My World." It is a place where creativity is unrestricted, enabling us to go beyond the constraints of the real world. Here, we may imagine worlds populated with strong individuals, dramatic music, seductive ladies, and even philosophical ideas customised to our preferences.
It provides a break from the routine of daily life and serves as a playground for our creative spirit.

"My World" is a place of reflection, subjectivity, and profoundly meaningful individuality. It is a place where our opinions and subjects may find shelter as well as a place where our feelings and ideas interact to determine how we see the world.

> "***Within the sanctuary of 'My World.'***
> ***the boundaries of understanding expand infinitely.***
> ***It is a universe where individuality flourishes,***
> ***and the stars of thought and emotion illuminate the darkest corners of existence***"

In this world, we are freed from the restrictions of social expectations and are able to freely express our uniqueness.
It is a haven where imagination and creativity flourish, giving one a chance to escape the ordinary and express oneself.
A greater sense of fulfilment, authenticity, and a rich inner

life that adds depth and purpose to our existence can result from honouring and growing our own worlds as we traverse life.

ALONE vs loneliness

Even though the phrases alone and loneliness are sometimes used interchangeably, their connotations and meanings are different. Aiming to highlight the value of quiet and isolation, this philosophical theory compares the nature of being alone and feeling lonely. It does this by using metaphors, examples from real-life situations, and passages from literature and fauna.

Alone: Ignoring the Entire World

It is conceivable to see choosing to be by oneself as a purposeful choice to temporarily or permanently cut oneself off from the outer world. One can focus on reflection, self-discovery, and personal growth when they have purposefully distanced themselves from external influences. A condition of emancipation and freedom from society expectations is symbolised by the eagle's soaring high in the sky, just as it does on its own. People may rise above the world's clamour and diversions thanks to it, which gives them a wider view of the world and life.

In accordance with the scenario given, picture a creative individual finishing off their job in a peaceful studio. In this state of seclusion, they disengage from the outside world, enabling the free development of their creativity and the uninhibited voicing of their inner voice.

Loneliness: Whole-World Leaving You

However, loneliness is a subjective emotional state in which a person has a sense of isolation or estrangement from others despite being surrounded by other people. It is a severe case of loneliness that affects one's physical and mental well-being. A wounded wolf separated off from its pack is a metaphor for loneliness when it comes to metaphorical character. As it laments the loss of its buddies, it tries to find solace in being by itself. Similar to this, when one yearns for empathy and connection, loneliness may be a terrible condition.

For instance, Consider someone who feels alienated from the group and is unable to communicate or share their opinions and feelings. Even if they are physically there, they nevertheless feel alone because they think that everyone else has abandoned them.

Alone vs. Lonely:

Differentiating States and Emotions The difference between being alone and feeling lonely must be understood. While loneliness is a psychological condition of feeling distant or alone from people, regardless of their presence, being alone refers to the physical state of seclusion.

Better to be by oneself in serenity than to be surrounded by confusion.

The Calm Lake and the Desolate Island as a metaphor Imagine a serene lake surrounded by luscious vegetation as a metaphor for solitude. The lake is unaffected by outside forces and continues to be peaceful and calm. A lonely island among a stormy sea, on the other hand, represents desolation. The island has a tattered, lonely, and cut off feeling from the outside world.

In example.

The Content Introvert:

An introverted person may decide to use their free time by engaging in activities that make them happy and satisfy their needs. They are content to be alone and find solitude to be enjoyable. However, despite being surrounded by others, a lonely extrovert may not have the fulfilling interactions they want for, leading to a persistent sense of loneliness.

How can one dislike and defeat loneness?

Self-improvement, introspection, and discovering one's strengths and hobbies may all happen while one is alone. It promotes self-reliance, certainty, and tranquilly inside. On the flip side, loneliness may be harmful, resulting in pessimistic views, a lack of vitality, and a need for meaningful relationships.

In **Metaphorical illustration, The Blossom of the Flower,** Being alone may be compared to a flower that thrives and blooms because it is left on its own in a peaceful garden. Because of its capacity to consume food internally in the quiet, it blooms vividly. Loneliness, on the other hand, is like a flower that has been neglected and robbed of the care it needs, leading it to wither and lose its brightness and

The Adventurer's Journey, for **instance**.

A person who sets out on a solo expedition views being by themselves as a chance to learn about themselves and develop their resilience. They overcome obstacles by drawing on their inner fortitude and developing a strong bond with nature.

In contrast, a lone traveller can find each step of the way to be tiresome and unable to fully enjoy the wonder and beauty all around them.....

In this case study of observation,

Alone and **loneliness** differ in that the former refers to a conscious decision to cut oneself off from the outside world while the latter refers to an emotional state of feeling cut off. While conquering loneliness necessitates a greater comprehension of oneself and a quest for meaningful relationships, accepting one's aloneness may promote personal development and self-assurance.

In the midst of a busy world, one may find fulfilment and tranquilly by recognising the beauty of isolation.

YOU-DO-YOU

Each individual is saddled with responsibility for their own choices, actions, and survival at the very heart of who they are. Excuses could offer momentary comfort, but taking responsibility for one's actions and working hard to overcome obstacles in life is the true path to success and satisfaction. A person is solely responsible for every choice they make, every problem they encounter, and every resolution they come up with. Placing blame on external factors or making up justifications to avoid taking responsibility only hinders development and self-awareness. This philosophical perspective emphasises the importance of living a proactive life and accepting responsibility for one's actions. Think of yourself as the ship's captain, navigating the vast ocean of life, using the metaphor from "Captain of Your Ship." Your boat can be pushed under your control, its course may be changed as needed, and it can resist any weather. Personal responsibility requires taking the helm and guiding your ship with tenacity and fortitude.

For instance,

"The life of Nelson Mandela is a great illustration of accepting personal accountability. Despite spending years in an unfair jail, he resisted letting resentment or justifications determine his course. Instead, he accepted responsibility for his actions, made the most of his time in jail by learning, fortifying, and ultimately leading South Africa out of apartheid."

Numerous physical and psychological obstacles are presented to us in life; it is up to us to learn from them and adjust in order to withstand them and prosper. We get the information and skills required for our trip by actively interacting with the components that are accessible.

Think of yourself as a gardener taking care of the garden of your life. The soil has to be actively cultivated, knowledge seeds need to be sown, growth needs to be nurtured, and impediments need to be removed to allow for progress to be made. Your life is a vibrant ecosystem, and everything you do affects it. Marie Curie exemplifies the power of active engagement. As a pioneering scientist, she took responsibility for her intellectual pursuits and made significant contributions to the fields of physics and chemistry. Through her tireless work and dedication, she revolutionized scientific understanding, earning Nobel Prizes in both disciplines.

As the saying goes,

"The only man who never makes a mistake is the man who never does anything."

-Roosevelt Theodore

This quote from Theodore Roosevelt emphasises the idea that action always involves making mistakes and failing. It encourages people to embrace personal responsibility and draw lessons from their experiences rather than dodging issues by making excuses.Accepting complete responsibility for our means and actions of survival is the cornerstone of personal growth and happiness. By recognising our duty as the captains of our own ships, actively interacting with life's components, and drawing inspiration from historical knowledge, we may cruise our courses with integrity, resiliency, and a commitment to self-improvement.

Though temporary consolation may be found in excuses, real empowerment comes from accepting personal responsibility and the opportunities that come with it.

The WoRLd iS OpEn foR InTErPrETaTIoN

Sorry to break it to you,
but it's not always the case when you think that some unknowable act is causing anything to happen.
Our cosmos and the reality in which we live are constantly subject to interpretation.

The statement "The world is open for interpretations" implies that the planet's nature permits many viewpoints and interpretations. It recognises that human experiences, perceptions, and understanding are inherently diverse. The world itself offers countless opportunities for interpretation, just as various people each interpret works of art or literature in their own special ways.
This openness results from the complexity and intricate nature of existence, where numerous contexts, influences, and circumstances interact to affect our perception of reality.

In the vast wilderness of existence, every person transforms into a wanderer in search of a destination. Similar to how a hiker uses their senses and intellect to explore a forest and encounter a variety of topographies, flora, and animals, we navigate our surroundings utilising both of these senses. There is always room for interpretation in every contact and every occurrence.

Similar to hikers, we encounter several pathways that lead to fresh ideas, emotions, and perspectives. Like the bright colours of a forest, our perceptions give the world around us greater depth and complexity.

Despite this openness, we still have knowledge gaps to overcome. Nobody is aware of every possibility, hence nothing is known about what may happen. This quote emphasises how unpredictable and uncertain life is by nature.We can never fully understand every aspect of life, despite our greatest efforts. In the same way that an explorer could unintentionally stumble onto a secret grove in the forest, we might come across events and phenomena that are beyond our comprehension.

Imagine an investigation by a group of scientists into a complex setting, such as a coral reef. Each researcher contributes their own expertise, theories, and hypotheses to better comprehend the complex mechanisms of this underwater ecosystem. But despite their combined knowledge, there are still a lot of parts of the reef that haven't been found or studied. Through study, observation, and conversation, we are continuously adding to our understanding of the reef, but we are also constantly reminded of the vast mysteries that remain a mystery to us.

The expression "the world is open for interpretations" alludes to the variety and depth of human perception, where each individual contributes their own unique viewpoint to the fabric of reality.

But the adage "Nobody knows what all things can happen since nobody knows what all things can happen" serves as a sobering reminder of the boundaries of our understanding and the pervasive unpredictability of existence. It encourages us to approach the world with curiosity, humility, and an awareness of the mysteries that exist outside the realm of our understanding.

The exciting way to kill yourself

There are N many methods to physically end your life, ranging from painful gunshots to painless panting, but it's not the physical method that matters to me; it's the highest level of mind.

To "from the things we want to do" from "the things we have to do"

The two words that are the focus of internal conflict are those that were just described.

One finds opportunities and justifications to abandon his labour of love on the precise same day that he passes away. Because I truly believe that everyone should live their lives as fully as they possibly can.

Passion is the enemy of reason.

For this reason, it is only a diversion and a temptation that divert us from the course we need to be on.

The conflict between "wanting to do" and "having to do" is a fundamental paradox that people commonly encounter in their lives. It represents the tension that arises when one must fulfil obligations and responsibilities that are imposed by outside forces while still acting on one's sentiments and desires.

In order to better understand the complexities of this conundrum, this philosophical research delves into it, explores its implications, and offers examples from ordinary life, relevant situations, and quotes.

Our deepest aspirations and what is required of us from the outside don't line up, and here is where conflict occurs.

The distinction between "wanting to do" and "having to do" is that the former describes our actual objectives, aspirations, and wants, whilst the latter describes the demands made on us by society in terms of its duties, expectations, and commitments. Leonardo da Vinci, known for his creative and intellectual brilliance, struggled to reconcile his many interests with society norms. He excelled in many areas due to his wide variety of interests, but he frequently found it difficult to reconcile his creative goals with patron expectations and social conventions.

Even if a complete resolution of this conflict may not be possible, being aware of its complexity aids in making informed decisions and finding a workable middle ground. In the end, to resolve this conflict, one must be self-aware, prioritise, and be open to novel ideas that satisfy both internal and exterior requirements.

Stones And Sticks

In regards to the overall concept of observative analysis, the book WAR BETWEEN STONES AND STICKS is all about observing and analysing the emotional and logical components, out of which the subjective component of my choice or consideration helped me to be spookedly excited every day in terms of working, thinking, and decision-making.

Here, stones stand in for or resemble the illogical, emotive, sentimental, and emotional parts, whereas sticks stand in for or resemble the rational, logical, and stuff elements.

Conflict between sticks and stones, The entire thesis of the title is a claim made by Metophar that I advanced, with the exception of a partial thesis of perceptive observations about a dispute that no one could perceive.

Despite In my opinion, despite their shape and makeup, stones can support a sizable amount of weight. This was in contrast to emotional reflection, which frequently happens at random and can be placed on top of one another unwittingly or blatantly like stones on top of one another. The sticks on the other side can stand in for a person's capacity to think logically and rationally, as well as their credibility, and they are difficult to stack one on top of the other or stack simply.

The intense merging of the emotional elements and the exact resemblance of the instrument led me to believe that this similarity was sufficient. This effort to group all of the book's subjects connected to the inner mind under one chapter as one theme is intended to emulate and connect them all.

www.ingramcontent.com/pod-product-compliance
Lightning Source LLC
LaVergne TN
LVHW040952150826
845672LV00002B/665

* 9 7 9 8 8 9 1 3 3 0 6 4 1 *